FOR NOW

FOR NOW

EILEEN MYLES

THE 2019 WINDHAM-CAMPBELL LECTURE

YALE UNIVERSITY PRESS
NEW HAVEN AND LONDON

The *Why I Write* series is published
with assistance from the Windham-
Campbell Literature Prizes, which
are administered by the Beinecke Rare
Book and Manuscript Library at
Yale University.

Yale University Press books may be
purchased in quantity for educational,
business, or promotional use.
For information, please e-mail
sales.press@yale.edu (U.S. office) or
sales@yaleup.co.uk (U.K. office).

Printed in the United States
of America.

Library of Congress Control
Number: 2020934232
ISBN 978-0-300-24464-9
(hardcover : alk. paper)
ISBN 978-0-300-26141-7
(paperback)

A catalogue record for this book is
available from the British Library.

10 9 8 7 6 5 4 3 2 1

for Erin

FOR NOW

I think last year I got the beautiful bound versions Yale published of Patti Smith and Knausgaard giving this talk and I sat in a chair in my apartment and I took a look at each of them and at least as far as the beginnings both of them sounded like themselves and I thought well I certainly can do that.

When I received the invitation to give this talk, I think it was the summer before last or maybe that spring I was given a date and a fee and I kind of put it at the back of my mind as something nice that would happen the following September or October and then in August I got in touch with Michael because I hadn't heard anything but it turns out that's because I had the wrong year. And I figure I can start with that.

And I'll return to it now and again. 2018's talk would have been different and 2019 has been a chaotic and exceptionally beautiful year, right, crowded with incident (horrible) and time itself had a kind of optic quality (full of great and awful things to see and the year has been busy getting copied — that way being memorable) and these are the things I'm always feeding into my purpose which is to write and maybe to get this part over with right away — because I need an alibi.

I have a very definite feeling that I am simply living and how would that be possible if you also had a kind of ambition and fewer and fewer concrete plans as you moved out of childhood wanting to discharge it.

Alibi of course implies a kind of "elsewhere" and as you translate it into many languages it remains alibi, what's the word for alibi in Czech. It's alibi.

I have been arming myself with philosophies for years that support the notion that the point is to be here, to be present which I think is the truly hard part, and yet I keep coming back to it, it's undeniably true and writing it turns out is the easiest way to copy that feeling. I have been doing it for years.

I would like to be here, I think I'm here, and the more I write, and the more you read it the more it's simply a fact.

So that's pretty much done and now I'm living here.

The second detail pertaining to the invite I received to give this talk is that I have been living in an apartment in New York for forty-two years so that's where most of my life has occurred. My living, my thinking, my copying. It's one of those East Village rent stabilized apartments and my building had just been sold in 2017 for the umpteenth time and pretty soon after my lease was up I guess probably in June and the new landlady *totally* took her time getting the new lease to me, actually all of us, which of course spelt danger and finally I got an email from her, my landlady, Elaine Moosey, saying she wanted to meet each one of us to hand us our leases and I thought that's sweet and a few weeks later she's standing right there in my apartment. She's a conservative looking woman I bet about ten years younger than me and as soon as she got inside here, apartment 3C, she goes I'll give you 75,000 to leave. That's a visitor right. I chuckled and rejected her offer and she went on to say that she *knows* that as well as living here in the small very inexpensive apartment I also have a house in Marfa Texas. Which is not illegal, but a fact. And that she Elaine Moosey knows it.

I'm being watched. That was the feeling I got. Then she asked me what I do and I said I'm a writer

I didn't say poet which was interesting I generally do say that because it is far more perverse people generally don't know what a poet does but in the moment with my landlady I also grabbed a fat book of poetry out of a brown box sitting there right next to the tub and I flashed it even thinking maybe it would be nice to give her one (also wondering if there was anything incriminating in it) and she looked right through the two of us, my book and I, and then she said smiling wouldn't you rather write in Texas.

It's always very unpredictable where you will receive counseling in your life. There's a philosophy that everything is a gift. If everything were coffee that might be true. The implication is that Elaine Moosey my landlady is a gift. Me getting the year wrong was a gift. And certainly I'm talking to you the poets and writers and thinkers who are getting a nice check today. Nobody knows what it is Donald and Sandy have actually done by giving you this gift. You'll know right away of course but in some other way you won't know for years.

Every gift is mysterious. I met Donald Windham at the Ear Inn in the late seventies early eighties. He read for Tim Dlugos. Did you know Tim. He was one of those people who would close his eyes tight and go Eileen you *have* to come hear Donald Windham read from his memoir. That's when he would close his eyes and twinkle. He's great. And he was.

But actually I'm still thinking about the utter banal Buddhism of my landlady giving me advice and it's too bad we couldn't have had an actual conversation about it cause I genuinely *do* prefer to write in Texas and that's why I have my house but I will never leave my apartment on E. 3rd St. because this is my home that I love, I love the sweet worn quality of my apartment, historic stove, ancient sinks. Were people shorter in the past or was that how landlords needed to treat them. I have all this ludicrous cabinetry in my kitchen basically underneath which is the Tenement Museum. I keep thinking about Russia cause that's what it's like. Russia in the 90s was deeply worn. It was almost a colour. I went to a place called Lenfilm in Petersburg with my girlfriend in 1995 and the very step into that historic building was the most humanized step I had ever seen. So soft and rounded. And so is my building, my block, the excitement of it, the relentless filth of the city, the subway, and all that surrounds 2nd Ave., the F, long long and the changing crowds, and all the historic and present machinations of the City of New York, the apparatus of it and this weird guarantee, this built in security, this incredible fact of rent stabilization that saw me, the most generalized seeing, and knows me and generally has kept my rent low for so many years, and I mean my rent is really low, so low it's almost pornographic, just imagine. I can show you the poem: "the city of New/York has given me a [lifetime] rent stabilization/grant," I actually have used that line — it's like having a trust fund, a trust fund for the lower and the working classes and there's plenty of wealth here in New York jostling helplessly with the poor but the city has taught me almost everything I know about language and existence and being a writer, density of impression etc. etc. of the forms and identities and textures that assault and excite and distract me living here but that's not what I'm talking about here yet, probably never, I'm really talking about the legal and political conditions my conditions that created me as a writer and I mean largely low rent and thereby time because one gives on the other and how do you use it.

It really takes so much time to become a writer and you have to be able to roll in time itself, that was my experience, it seems to me, like a dog likes to roll in dead fish at the beach. Or a dog (my dog) stands in the shit of a stable underneath the body of a horse (trembling) and feels awe. Cause there's so much shit and there's so much horse. But if you're somebody that wants to do that with your life which is just waste your time moment to moment, I mean it's great, I thought I will waste it being a poet, I threw the gauntlet down and what happened after that was nothing and nothing is where I work.

I'll get to the why of it. I think literature is wasted time, I don't think there's anything good about it. It's not a moral project except in this profound aspect of wasting time. I have had this adventure in all of these ways. It's the great adventure of our time.

I guess you could be in this position by being wealthy, or having a rich partner though I don't think being wealthy you would feel the same desperate intensity about living in this tiny preserve as one does if you're being poor and you found yourself in a situation like mine that was simply a convergence of class and history and culture and on a personal level lethargy, fear and procrastination so that you wound up there somewhere workable where you could simply live and then you simply couldn't move because where in the world was as cheap as New York if you lived among the class that lives this way (I suppose I'm talking about negative awe) and all of that became your decor to some extent even involuntarily relishing the fabric of being poor I could tell you endless jokes about it but I'm not going to do that now and I wasn't alone in it, my condition, there was an us to it. Now there's about three left and when I go there'll be two.

My apartment is pathetic. It's an aerie from which I look down. From my 300 sq. foot apartment, from the position of bed I literally espy the New York Marble Cemetery, a graveyard from the 19th C. which has been sort of like being young and then not so young and holding a skull for all these years and in that fragile and elevated space I read and wrote and just kind of looked at things very very slow.

And my built-in bed is jammed right up against the window and I sleep on my right side, and anywhere in the world if I can't sleep, if I can't remember what sleep is or how it works I just think of the window. It is the original. I know it's not very American to have a home. To feel this way about a location at all. But this is the time I am in.

Dogs as we have learned shit in relation to the magnetic poles of the earth. So, shrug.

I went to the ruins in Mexico in 1985 and in the Anthropological Museum I discovered a writer, John L. Stephens, who wrote a book called Incidents of Travel in Central America, Chiapas and Yucatan.

There were a series of similarly named books. Through him I became enamored with the idea of becoming a travel writer of which he was among the first. Later I discovered Robert Smithson and his Incidents of Mirror Travel in the Yucatan. Obviously he was responding to Stephens, to Mexico and his own condition of coming from postindustrial suburban New Jersey. Using stuff. He started off being a writer but wound up more of a sculptor, conceptual artist, an earth artist. He made big and little things outside and often he took pictures of them and installed versions of the entirety inside. His response to Mayan antiquity was to put tiny mirrors in it. He *was* a poet after all. I had no access to this graveyard for a very long time. I just had a view.

Once I drunkenly climbed over the fence with my girlfriend and laid down on the raised gravestones and drank our beers and looked at the stars.

By around 2010 the Marble Cemetery began opening on the first Sunday in the month May through October I recommend it and also a historic plaque has magically appeared on the metal gate and I discovered that John L. Stephens' remains are down there and had been right below my window for thirty years. And only last year on the teevee show The Billions Axe and Wags were standing down there in the dark of my computer warm on my stomach in bed. Wags was buying a plot. The contortions of here and elsewhere are endless and rich.

Even Robert Smithson had a name for it, all the mirrors and the remembering and the displacement. Ultramodernism. And this is what I do about that.

It's a literature of tiny folds, of nothing and then a lot.

I'm wondering if everyone has a childhood conducive to becoming an artist except that childhood is that somehow, the original studio, the time place, you make art sometimes and they the people in school try and make you write.

Everybody doesn't like it; I did though I didn't think there was anything to it. Writing as a profession? Wouldn't you want the world?

It's interesting we got around to this. I had other thoughts in mind but as a kid the important fact is that you radically understand your own condition. You know that you don't have to go to work or pay bills and everything's new so there's an enormously liberated feeling which certainly abuts on this awesome space which is writing or art or rolling in the shit of time.

Though let me add: this singular experience I project onto childhood the romance I have about dwelling in poor spaciousness from approximately my mid-twenties to my mid-forties contains a genuine element of risk but not of condemnation, because the lives I collided with when I went out opened capacities and spaces and wider and wider opportunities if only I continued walking and breathing and picking up the phone and if I were so broke that the phone was turned off I could go downstairs to the bodega to call John Ashbery and ask him if he would recommend me for an emergency grant and because I had such entitlement (I *knew* about this grant) and had written some good poems I'm standing here right now whereas some of my neighbors in my building came to New York from other countries, continents or territories (our colonies!) Puerto Rico and six people lived in the apartment right next door to my one, and the child of that house is now a large man who doesn't leave the block or hardly the building his name is Steve and a woman on the third floor I love who has been carrying her groceries up the stairs bump bump bump in a cart for years we're probably the same age and she came here from South America to get an operation for her son (whereas our government is now pulling such kids out of the hospital and deporting them) and later in college he was a camp counselor and he wrote some emails to one of the campers after the summer that he got in trouble for and he actually went to jail and he came back much bigger (jail big) than he was before maybe he committed a crime but I think it was because he was brown and his mother lived her life for him so I have to acknowledge for myself that I am living outside of that level of suffering.

I wasted time absolutely like I knew I should, well I could. The waste was like a frame, an award. An attainment. Literature is waste for sure. But the award was just time itself.

There are writers who have jobs, they probably had children and they had to get up at dawn to write for an hour and that's not me. Queerness is a factor. Even in childhood you're a bit of a fraud. And later you just want to put all that time back.

If I had that little time (like the ones who write in the morning) I don't know what I would have said. And a lot of those people were women. I didn't want kids and I didn't want a job. I knew that if I had either one of those things I would think about them all of the time. It would set my morning and it would set my night. I would be in its clock, its childhood and its adolescence, its responsibilities. I think women are supposed to open their legs to time and let it pass through them. It strikes me that that's what choice is all about. If a man chooses to put sperm inside of a woman inside of her it must stay. It's like she's Tupperware. The problem is she's visible. And there are women who want to have babies and I feel awe for the women who make that choice. In fact I have been overwhelmed by the generosity of women lately. I was getting on a ferry in July, or I was trying to make a ferry and I stumbled and fell down and I managed to get on the ferry nonetheless but what was amazing was that in the café area of the boat where I was triumphantly putting a band aid on my bruises, my hands were bleeding from falling and one woman looked at me and said they have first aid here. Oh I've got a band aid I told her. Yeah I see I'm just telling you in case you need more. Thank you. It was nice that she was following me with her eyes. In a few minutes I realized I would really like an ibuprofen and I asked her if she had one and she said I don't. But she really looked at me and another woman right over there said I've got one and she started digging in her bag and then the first woman said no I do, I do I do and she handed a couple to me happily and the other woman said patting her bag I've got them if you need more.

I'm good I said and I sat down and I was hurting a little bit but it was incredible to feel so seen.

These women could do anything with their lives beyond care and seeing but there is that part, a practice, which is ingrained in females and everyone takes it for granted and even despises women a little bit for it. Men do for sure and women do too it's the down gender but I'm gaining a new respect for how it's amazing in small ways and large ways how people and especially women are in the condition all over the world of caring more and largely they are keeping people, mostly small people and male people too they are being kept alive by the caring efforts that are considered no great prize except if you fell down and believe me right now everything is falling but you felt the deep simple pleasure of being seen. I was brought up to be that way too but I kind of ran away from home I left Boston and everything that would have shepherded me that way in my twenties because I needed all the time in the world. I wanted to taste it once. I didn't even know if it even existed. I went to Europe and it wasn't there. Was it in the past. San Francisco didn't have it either. Once I tasted time I never wanted anything else. And that is what I'm doing here. The only way I can prove it is that I started writing. Writing is my alibi. A few things must be true.

Eileen had the wrong year. Around the time that I received the invitation to create an alibi I also received an eviction notice. By now my building had cameras on every floor and at the front door and I think they decided they had enough information on me to pry me out of my apartment and they claimed I didn't live there anymore. But I did.

I got a lawyer, David, and he agreed to take my case and then he told me that the worst possible scenario was that it could take a year or two and we would possibly go to court how much will that cost I asked him and then he quoted what to my mind was a considerable sum for his labors on my behalf and I said alright I guess it's worth it and the next day I got invited to give this talk and they offered me the same figure my lawyer had quoted as the maximum legal fee so I thought somebody is writing this it seems and obviously it is me now. So I thank you.

I'm listening to a train I'm crazy about in Marfa Texas the train is largely why I came here. It goes crashing through the blue it's an entirely different energy than New York. I've been writing in Texas all along just like Elaine Moosey suggested I would like but I pretended I was in New York because weirdly it would feel less gross this way.

I think I must elaborate in some detail on this thing about copying. I'm in Europe right now and so I'm writing in that kind of English. I remember being young and it was Christmas and I had a large drawing pad and a charcoal pencil and we were all waiting for my father and hoping I think that he wouldn't come home drunk. So I was making the tree. I wasn't normally a detail person but I decided the way I could handle the excitement and the fear of the moment was to copy the tree, each needle one by one and I could show it to my father when he came home. I don't think it went well that night and I don't think I even remember finishing the tree but I remember copying and that it calmed me down and gave me a relationship to the world. I want *that*. I remember going to Mass Art when I was a senior in high school for an interview maybe and a test. I remember sitting in a room in a building that was filled with the smells of paint and the sounds of people making things and we went into a room and a female model her breasts half exposed was sitting on a pedestal with drapes and I thought wow and I drew her. I didn't go to art school but I always wanted to do what they do and I know that their practice is complicated and diverse but I contend that somewhere in there is this action of copying. Holding perhaps. I take pictures of my apartment and put it on IG, I take pictures of my dog. An abstract piece of light moving across the room fills me with something that commands that I copy. I was on a boat last weekend I began a new notebook and I started noting the water and the line of the trees on the shore, and the dots of houses and the waving lines of the boat over our head. It doesn't feel gross when I do it, well maybe a little and I urged Erin to join me copying everything (in words) which is a form of loving the world, aiming and choosing, I suppose just the way it is. Life is I do this.

If you ask me to tell you why I write it probably has to do with this deep comfort/discomfort of being in the world and this option of devotion. If I want to sit here and copy all day that might be the best option available to me, it's not an anti-depressant and it's not exhilarating and it's not aerobic but it is a form of chanting and I do do it for religious reasons. I mean it's my default position.

What I think about a lot is how when I was young I don't remember feeling at all but I have these pictures like the one of drawing the tree. So what's not gross for example is to copy an experience you can easily summon up from memory (putting in the feeling perhaps) and as the tape winds down you might pop in a bit of contemporary material that you can copy right in front of you. It kind of makes a bump like the first time I heard guitar frets on a recording, or the first time somebody laughed casual in the recording studio Dylan or Bobby Darin men I loved who sang and then they sang the present as well. They gave you this little bit of stuff. I was thrilled by the naked admission of these two things next to each other and if I love a thing eventually I will use it. I will slip it in when it signals the experience of presence even if it's the present at the front of my mind. The experience of standing here is extremely weird in that I was asked to come in 2018 and a year passed and there was a vague thought of *this* moment all of that time, and eventually the one thought which was that I had the wrong year and then sitting in Texas trying to create a script for this moment (in a house with a dog and particular weather) and then looking at it in New York and saying nah but enjoying say the artificial here's an indication that I carry the apartment I'm sitting in now (then) in my head. I have been in hell lately about my apartment.

It is the repository of now but it is a sick little Eileen museum. Where's the goddamn plaque. It's a small space with a thick feel. I think it's a hot space.

I think you can have sex in it. There's a dirty public private feeling to it all. It's been used and used and used. By me and before me.

I think I've been taking photographs of it since 2018 because I know that I'm leaving. You've got to go. I don't mean legally but that part gets confused. What do we own? Obviously I was just going to fight the mother fuckers how dare they think they can get rid of me, the most famous poet in the east village at this moment a neighborhood of many moments now this. I want a plaque and this is that.

> The floors in my apartment are nice old wood. There's a tree outside the window and in summer its shaking green leafiness acted like curtains that softened the hungover mornings and allowed the darts of light in the later afternoon to illuminate my place. Sometimes in the afternoon friends would come by and we'd drink red drinks, hot ones. By the fall the leaves were down and I began to think of my apartment as blue. It's warmer now, everything having gone around twice. Chris used to live here. For a couple of years. There's a character now

called Eileen's apartment and perhaps she remembers everything I don't.

(from *Chelsea Girls*)

Someplace in the spring May in fact I went to court to begin the fight to keep my place. The court mainly doesn't want you to go to court so they encouraged us to settle.

It's a funny word right. Somebody was talking about the person they were dating who was becoming unavailable but he described it to her as he needed to settle. What does that mean. That he is a foreign country to himself. That he is occupying another's land. Is he his own man?

The fight to that point had been interesting. My landlord contended I was always in Marfa when I left my apartment. It used to be that if you had a rent stabilized apartment you had to be in your bed half the nights of the year. They didn't want any rich person who was NOT using the place to maintain occupancy. No pied-à-terre please. Which just means foot on the ground. Is that how I use this. Is that true.

Apparently the apple cart of landlords was upset a few years back when a travelling shoe salesman won his case. His point being that he travelled for work so it was unjust that he be penalized when he was simply going to work. So if you can demonstrate that your travel is for work then you may stay in your apartment. So the cameras demonstrate that I am coming and going all the time for instance I was going this week to Berlin and Brussels. And now I am in New Haven. My landlord contends that I am only going to Marfa and if that was the case, if I was there more than here this would be illegal.

I have proved through cell phone records and ATM records that I am in many locations beyond New York and TX and they want more detail to that effect which is when I threw up my hands and they were offering me money and I thought I'll go.

They asked for a figure and I gave a large one and they gave a significantly smaller one in response and I snorted and carried on and when I got home I thought uh. I looked around at the light and all the books. Here again. And again and again and again. So I communicated to my landlady via my lawyer David that I would go.

All summer I have been going. The leaves have been shaking outside my window, probably the most beautiful window view in New York. Each cruddy step up my stairs, each crack on the wall. I was in San Francisco with my friend Jocelyn and she said Eileen I don't think you should let go of your apartment. She said New York walls are so bumpy. She indicated the smoothness of the walls in her house in San Francisco. You can fix it. I was staying with her for a couple of days. Kevin Killian had died. There was a memorial.

My friends are dying now. Barbara Barg died last summer. Tim died in 1990 but that was AIDS and that was too much.

I said I don't want smooth walls. I like bumpy walls. I want the past. Not mine, somebody else's. I had already decided to move to East Harlem and then I walked around a little and decided I didn't know anybody up there. I decided it had to be in this neighborhood or Chinatown. I went to see an apartment in Chinatown that was on a great street and the building was great and the kitchen was great and so was the bathroom and then the front room just stopped. All the windows faced other buildings so there was light but it was abbreviated and the train was nearby so the apartment shook.

All the apartments in Chinatown and most of the ones I saw in pictures on the internet were versions of what I already had but all gussied up. It was sad. They had destroyed all our little apartments and now they wanted 3500 bucks for the crime. I had decided I would get someplace huge for a year or two, just waste the money so what.

But that felt wrong. Then Max who I had just missed at MacDowell where I went for an abbreviated stay this summer because I needed to find an apartment, I heard Max and Sarah's apartment in Brooklyn which they were leaving was huge. I had ruled out Brooklyn.

The papers came through from the landlord one day, I had only to sign on the dotted line, I was doing it and I was going crazy inch by inch. I am leaving my home. Is anyone forcing me to do this. You are manipulating yourself said David who is not my lawyer but my therapist.

Max writes and says the other person didn't take the apartment if you are interested. I walked through it for five minutes I said sure. The apartment is gigantic, room after room a little dark with all this Somerville wood trim and doors and crystal knobs and overhead lamps like flower cups. Not exactly me but immense and I can have my 70th birthday party here. I had my 50th birthday in a loft in Times Square but if I further elaborate on that situation I'll be endangering my apartment. I'll take it I said. Crown Heights. Why not. I thought of Jean-Michel Basquiat — that kind of crown.

Writing and drawing, drawing and writing. Copying copying copying. God. God being something that happens in the repetition. Again and again. I have to love it in the language in order for it to be true. My contract with the world and with god. My god.

A week later when I really really needed to sign the paper and Max and Sarah said I could spend an hour in their apartment and get the feel actually a psychic had recommended this. Will I leave my home. I imagine them coming in with an enormous wrecking ball. Unpeeling me. I sat on the floor. I wandered down the long wooden corridor. I could write here in Sarah's office at the end of the enormous apartment where she had a green tree and I went home on the subway and thought not so bad and went into therapy and began to freak out. Do I have a good therapist?

Next morning I contacted David the lawyer and said I'm going to stay. Alright his folksy voice replied. We'll see what they say.

I thought about the movement in this area of my life, home which is where I began to write though it's not really this apartment, but the other apartment earlier in Soho I haven't even mentioned that place, Thompson Street, I guess that was where

I was actually alone for the first time in my life — I mean I guess where it didn't make me crazy, *that* was in San Francisco — but this apartment, the one on 3rd Street, had soul and a jungle out the window and even a myth.

Mary screamed. She was my neighbor when I moved into this building in 1977 and she had been a dancer and she lost her hand in a washing machine on East Sixth Street and now she had a hook and she had just settled her case and now she could leave. You have to go she screamed. This building is going to fall down on you. I really believed her and every time it shook in the night for forty-two years I thought it's ready to go. When I thought I was leaving I was sure it would fall down right after I left and I would shake my head over a cup of coffee and go I really knew something.

People would send me texts late at night, Delphine Blue did that, saying don't go. Don't move to Brooklyn. A cheap apartment is good.

What's at the copy shop right now on E. 4th Street where I get my mail is a map of Brooklyn. I bought it online and thought I will put it on the wall in my new apartment because where the hell is Crown Heights. It is no closer to JFK or LaGuardia. How can that be.

In Texas I have a map of Texas on the wall in the kitchen. I assume everybody thinks it's corny but I like to know where I am.

There are so many little buzzing sounds in my apartment. It's a tiny place coming from both directions, sizzling in my ears. I have no doubt that I will go just not now.

By the time this is a book (a book called "For Now" I decided) this will all be resolved. Isn't that interesting? Meanwhile I am thinking of departures. Separation. Loss. Robert Smithson was a big man for me for a while. I think we're the same person. He liked that the Museum of Natural History had both spacemen and cavemen. Which is very much like the Flintstones and the Jetsons — two kinds of time I participate in. Flintstones is drawing. Jetsons is the advanced postmodern form of writing in which all the versions of copying even a single thought laid out in all its pictures can take hundreds and hundreds of pages of motion to make something truly fantastic occur. There are many kinds of awe.

I wrote a whole novel about becoming a poet in New York and at the time I was being an academic in San Diego AND returning desperately to New York as much as I could. People would look at me in the street like they do in New York. They'd say are you *here*. I mean I had been hearing people say this for twenty-five years but I took it very personal at that moment because I felt the city had created me as a writer and now in their idle remark they were potentially taking it away. Yes I'm here I snorted. Or someone would allude to the fact that they were coming to do a reading in San Diego and they would giggle in an email as people do I'm excited to see you in your new stomping grounds. Oh my god. The furor this unleashed in me. Nothing was worse than people trying to extract gigs from me now like I was an academic, an opportunity for them to be on the road. One friend was hired for a semester as a visiting writer and at dinner she got trashed and sort of began pontificating about her work like she was actually the visiting writer and it was necessary at all moments for her to fulfill the terms of her work. My displacement in San Diego made me feel very vulnerable though I know in my heart that you can write anywhere. I think though I wouldn't have become a writer if I didn't move to New York. I don't know if it's true but I like that story. I just momentarily had a hard time spelling the word fulfill. It looks wrong right.

Is Brooklyn New York. It's very political. I wonder about that now.

There are writers I know who never tell anyone when they travel that they are writers. People say what do you write. Why don't we like that. Or they say I always wanted to be a writer. Their eyes get kind of dreamy like the way photographers who take your picture are waiting for you to look. People think that you go to beautiful places to write and you're just living the life. And it's actually true. The part that sucks is that you're writing.

I was just thinking I've written enough and maybe I'll charge my computer for a while and pack. I'll write a note. And then I start getting ideas. Writing is like my sex life. What I am is abstract. I'm happy to seem the dumbest thing in the world and then I cut my eyes and wonder if you believe me. I've been doing what I consider not my work lately. Like I wonder what *this* is. Kind of in between I suppose. Is it noble to say why I write. Is it a gig.

But then do I have any religion at all. There's a point at which I don't care. And I'm there now. Dear Diary. I've turned out introductions to books by important writers and artists, mostly female, some living, some dead. I did Chantal Akerman, I did Kathy Acker, I did Gail Scott, I did Lynne Tillman. I did Can Xue. I did Michael Lally. With Michael I thought I had agreed to do a blurb. It's good to do things for men once in a while.

I only say yes when I can't resist but I can't resist too much. I'm always waiting to get here. Not here exactly, not Yale, but the place whether it's a poem or MY NOVEL that I consider MY WORK. But lately I've noticed a horrible thing. I almost prefer writing about the living and dead artists better. I've had enough of this. Not writing, but you know a telling that resembles a story that details aspects of a self strangely similar to mine. People might say that's because you don't write fiction. But I do. Do you think this is—I don't know—whatever it is that fiction isn't. When my hand hits the keyboard I'm lying.

All of it's an alibi. Because I am aware not so much that my own becoming a writer is a construction of sorts but more that there's a kind of aesthetic experience I believe that precedes the work so that you kind of fail into it finding your style and content and opportunity all together at last and that's happened enough times for me to believe that that's my process and it exists and will occur again no matter how much suffering my work causes me and betrayal is so deeply a part of it because I'll be sailing along thinking *this is incredible* and days later I'll stop and some version of me that lives at a different pace reads what I've written and pronounces it bad and I return to it later and pick out pieces and surges and rearrange it so ultimately I'm talking about ease and how *it* is an utter fiction so I disbelieve all ideas about genre because it's all such fabricated stuff, writing, art, music every bit of it is not so much lying but instead is perched in relation to this other thing which is living and however I am about it, doing this thing, in my case writing, makes that thing I think more beautiful. I have time for it. I am in it and I am relentlessly talking about time but I can feel it drumming, rarely am I really peaceful, no I'm happy but I'm digging this little hole right here which is really tearing a hole in the other thing, copying it somehow in a way I like and that lets me fall out and relax in a way that I hope is nothing like the writer drunk at dinner telling us her stuff.

★

I'm just going to catch you up.

I've written half. Actually that's not even true. I've written one-third. Which is horrifying. I'm in Texas. I expected to be writing this right after the new year and today I'd be done. By now I'd be doing *my* writing, that fuzzy category. (What is this if not that? Question marks are hysterical. I'll use one.)

I was supposed to be travelling today but I'm not. Everything's different. My girlfriend's sick so she can't travel anyhow. We were supposed to be in San Francisco and Miami. I decided just to stay here in Texas, now January 15th, and do this thing and maybe I'll just write the whole damn thing tonight. Who knows. I have plenty of ideas.

I'd like to get a diagram down about what's actually going on in my exact location—beyond the fact that I am not even supposed to be here — which is that in the big back yard behind my house I am building something. I've never built anything before. I've decided to call it the poet shack. It's an awkward thought that building out there. When I bought the place there was a lovely powder blue ruin in the yard, a building, with bushes around it I've taken many pictures of and posted on IG and people say in the comments section "looks like a painting," which embarrasses me but it's true. It's why I posted it. The kitchen window looking out is small and dirty and sometimes there's fog and the result is crazy. In August when I came here to write I would go out there in the afternoon. The ceiling was mostly gone and open to the sky and there were four big railroad ties for the building's posts and the rafters were torn and ragged not far above my head; the back wall was partially absent in a triangular shape and behind it I could see a tree.

I kept my meditation cushion in there and a little befouled buddha from San Diego (who fell off a table in California and his head came off and I stuck it back on with glue THEN I painted it over with gold glitter nail polish) and I would drag it all out into the afternoon sun even taking my shirt off. And Honey would sit there with me. It's such an abandoned neighborhood. I love it. Airbnb over there, often empty. Alley to my right where only an occasional truck stops and empties the dumpster and mostly nobody ever in that yard. So even though houses are close I never see anyone at all definitely not when I'm shirtless on my pillow talking to god. I mean that's what I'm doing now. It's you.

It was the first thing I wrote on my legal pad:

I had a
date with
god tonight

and then it gets more incoherent:

what [ate]
dumpster
diving
in my own
refrigerator

Meaning stayed in to write and I hadn't shopped. I stood repeatedly looking at the expiration date on the lettuce and then I thought if I was dumpster diving (which I've never done; I'm neither rich nor poor enough for it) of course I would eat this. I would think it was great *only three days past expiration.*

I mention the yard and the blue shack because of what happened when I was here in the fall — I was here in October and November not to do *this* but to really write. I was working on my new novel and in fact it was feeling pretty terrible. When I came back here in January (now) I could have started working right away on this, I should have, but I decided to read the novel instead and indeed it was really awful though some of it I thought was pretty good. I just didn't want to do this yet and I didn't have to — not until now. Time interestingly though has made it hot. Once there's a deadline the back of your mind comes shooting forward and the lazy front keeps litanizing and somehow the two like an old relationship are getting together. And hotter still, it's a return. That's the thing we talk about in therapy lately. At this point in life it's all about the return. And that feels right.

I was here in the fall and in a general sense I'd like to share that I have a lifelong obsession with detail. Somebody else might call it fetish. Like it's a funky coat but what I absolutely care about is the buttons. I decided that my very rough cement bathroom needed a porcelain toilet paper roll. I mean there's a real nostalgia in having a house. In an apartment you'd never put in a window. But that's exactly what you're doing here. It feels like you're doing "forever." I found a nice old school toilet paper roll on etsy but it arrived broken. It was from Canada the lady said she packed it very securely but customs opened the package, sniffed my toilet paper roll and threw it back into the box *outside* the bubble wrap. My friend in New York put the pieces together, messily, as I requested and it took about a year to find someone in Texas to attach it to the concrete wall. Jim (who had been fixing the fence so Honey wouldn't go wandering) turned me on to Jean Bell, a contractor who lives in Fort Davis, and has done stunt work, cattle ranching and so many other things and Jean knew exactly how to attach the fucker. As I was going through the yard with her showing my property we lit upon the shack. I told her I was going to fix that up someday. Well let's have a look.

I would say they are pretty close to done. It keeps getting more complex somehow. It will have a black toilet (which Erin tells me is so eighties. I just thought it was black) and a clawfoot tub because I spotted a couple of abandoned ones in a yard up the street. *A tub*. I got so excited. I left the guy notes for days. Finally he was tall, scratching in the doorway. I don't want to sell the tub.

I found one, right downtown & equally hard to locate its owner. Tubs are all over the place in this town, rarely plugged in. People are like that here. Earlier I had gone to a goat dairy where I looked at a rusty one for a hundred bucks but they directed me to mine just sitting against a wall in town. I don't even take baths so it's funny but something needed a tub in the middle of the growing shack, like some kind of super detail. Cool, right? Yeah said Jim.

Well now that they are almost done it is a little weird to have a small room in your yard, better heated and insulated than my house, don't know how that happened both my dog and I are by now very attached to them and Jim told me grinning that he and Jean were beginning to imagine a sister shack on the other side of the yard so they could just keep going.

When the little shack was in its original state the back wall that was mostly gone made a rough little triangle and I could see a young tree that was growing on the outskirts of my yard. Jean and I talked about building the place back up and she said that tree is going to be hard. See what you can do I said. Or something like that. When I returned a month later the place was pretty much flattened except for the four posts and her and Jim had cut down the tree.

I thought you guys had talked about that earlier he said when we were hanging out and he was vaping at the end of the day. We call him Minimum Jim cause he's a man of few words though he actually isn't. I guess there's a way in which I'm not entirely clear or I just don't understand and then I go away and something is gone.

I touch the raw wood of the little tree, a short stump that has enabled the rest of the house, I mean shack. Jean was telling me about this friend of hers who makes really cool triangles for up there near the arch and I said I'll just take one and the triangle hovers mysteriously now, waiting for glass and I am going to plant something later on to grow right into that space.

What Jim and Jean don't know is that what they have built in my yard is my apartment. I believe it is part of the return. There's no other reason for wanting a desk with a tub and some kind of bed which eventually it is. Bathing naked in my yard where nobody sees.

Now I actually think I am going to need some kind of trees or weeds or growing things over there. I was meditating in the shack today. It's cold, they weren't working.

I duplicate the apartment not because of its endangerment or some lack but just because I think it's practical. I've got a reference to it in my yard if I want to go home but stay in Texas. Here's the latest.

About the original, my east village pad. So, through the prodding questions and receptive looks from my therapist David, and really because of the pony-tailed agent who showed me a bad apartment one day in the thirties — right after therapy, that's how I finally arrived at my conclusion.

The place was wrought iron up the front steps and inside the tenants were running across the balcony with their breakfast plates and when I told her on the street about my apartment situation she asked what my rent was and she looked at me silent for a moment. She said if you don't have to leave don't go. People love that. That's pretty honest for a real estate agent. I know.

What I *also* haven't mentioned was that during the summer when I was still negotiating a buy out the law changed. New York in many ways is still a pro-tenant city unlike say Cambridge where I was born that took away rent control in the 90s and it's never been the same again. We need the poor, the alternative, the mess, whether we are them or not. We need them more than the rich frankly. The poor give life purpose. They make it visible.

The new rent law in New York says that when a landlord gets rid of a tenant like me who has lived in their place for 42 years they get a legal rent increase, a bump, for each of those years so think of it, evicting me would have brought Elaine Moosey a fortune. I stopped one of my fellow tenants in the hall one day. I said I'm Eileen. He said hi. Do you mind telling me what you pay. I just was curious. He told me. I said you know that's probably not even legal. I don't care, he said smiling. He was nice.

Evicting me now (after the law has changed) brings Elaine Moosey about eighty bucks more a month. What's incredible said David laughing is that she is still offering a buyout. She *really* wants you out.

So what happens now I asked. Once I told him I was planning to stay. I felt a shiver of excitement. Then a drop in energy.

We're going to court. I had been in the building; I had even been in the hearing room of the housing court but I had not yet gone to court and now I would.

In November I met with David and my landlord's lawyer Gabriel Finney, a former opera singer. I figured this would somehow make him sympathetic to me but this was not that show. After a lot of dallying we all entered the chambers and met our judge. This was still pretrial. She had a reputation for being a lefty said David. We talked, she asked me something about my writing. I said I was mainly a poet but I was working on a novel. She seemed to be taking me in. She was a good-looking woman in her fifties, smart thin featured. She was putting things in their correct contexts as she heard them. I liked her way.

She asked Gabriel why his client was still pursuing this you must know about the new law. I think he kind of shrugged she has family; you know kids and uh and with that the judge kept writing things and looking at her papers. She asked if the date (in December) was acceptable to us both. It was we agreed and we left.

About three weeks later I get an email from my lawyer telling me that my landlord had dropped the case and this was the end of that story.

It was a day before my birthday and the good news entered the antiphonal radiance. Look what happened in my sixties. I'd begun a new era now in which I was simply home again. This, I thought?

I've got to finish this piece. Erin's sick with a flu in my bed and I'm going to ask her how she feels about my apartment (she was very pro-moving) cause being sick is so rich in accidental information. The toilet gets blocked and the plumber hits on her. It doesn't have to be that way I point out. I want to defend her. He's such a good plumber she says. I think he should fix your sink.

It's forward to the past just like that. I almost have a little metal house in the yard. It looks like a train. I had them put stripes of the battered old blue tin at the bottom or in the middle of each wall of gleaming corrugated tin. Except for the front. Which is like reddish from the old roof. Do you need a drawing. I'm watching them work as I write.

I am really struggling against taking a nap. Just the act of writing inspires in me a deep thick sleep and when I arise I step off that other planet refreshed ready to write again whereas they finish work and they're tired, beat.

I don't know the difference between the mind and body or I do but I am always trying to erase it.

Or I plunder it supremely, some new thing, until it's empty then I move on.

I have a story. I'd like to start it in Marfa because that would explain how I got here, I mean Texas. And even why I am creating my apartment's double in my yard. I came to Texas in 2015 for a month and a couple of days before the end of the month I went to a going away party for Hilary, who I didn't know. She was friends with Brandon and Lisa who were my best friends that month and we went hiking and I generally did anything they proposed since they lived here. The house next door was empty. It had a very big yard and we were wandering around trying to get peeks of the inside of the house but it wasn't easy. A few days later I asked someone I met, Mary, who sold real estate if she would show me some stuff and the first place she brought me was that house so I made an offer and by the fall I was living there some of the time. Texas felt great because it was deeply unfamiliar, Marfa was an art town so there was something to do though it never felt like anyone cared if you did it. I bought the house as a single person. It was mine to write in, not a place that reflected the hopes of some relationship. I was no longer counting on that. I wanted my own future.

I had a girlfriend in the 90s who was a film-maker and when we got involved she told me the sad story that she had just been robbed. They took all her film equipment which was super 8. She lived on 14th street and robbery was a common thing. Be a poet I said. The implication being that we had nothing and you couldn't take anything away from me. It was a mean thing to say kind of though she did write too and honestly I wanted to make films, always did and poetry was a default profession. It was what I did because I had nothing and my gifts were invisible. Well not entirely.

I wrote on napkins and I wrote on cigarette packs and I wrote in tiny notebooks of all kinds and I wrote on legal pads. Ideally I wrote with a nice thick runny pen, a rolling writer, originally a pen-tel. It's moved on to being a Pilot G-2 10 otherwise known as bold. I like fine you might say. Well I pity you. What I like best about cartoonists is the lettering they do within the cartoon which is the world. The world is a balloon expanding and contracting with breath and you write when you feel that surface growing almost to notate the arc which is living breathing.

Light has taken a corner and you do it in sound. You do it broad and you do it funky, and you do it like a cartoon. I don't want to bore you with my history. I'm sick of my history. I'm trying to tell this nice and convey the experience of living and writing unreflected, simply in it and almost having a graffiti style toward existence, everything in a way is a public wall, even the most private expression gets hot on its own visibility once in a while. Am I getting too abstract. I'm saying the emphasis was on being not saving for a very long while and yet there was also a slow movement towards permanence. Helplessly. I moved into this apartment where I am sitting now and for a while I had a big drawing desk because my boyfriend Scott thought I could make money drawing cartoons (I was good) and possibly he didn't want to have to always buy all my drinks. In the far right hand corner of my desk was a black spring binder with a white label on it called the haps. I had previously lived on the upper west side and I would set the clock and make myself write and it was fucked. But a good poem would occasionally come through and I wouldn't have to fix it so much. Pushing a word here and there around. It would become one of my reading poems and early on my life in New York was a reading project. I would go out and read my poems to anyone. I have written about this before so this is the undetailed version.

This one's all sound even better that it's a writing project not a talking one. I am speaking silently here on my couch. Eventually poems became books. My first book was small published by the poet Jim Brodey. I had forgotten until this exact second but there was an original of that manuscript and I did the title page in sharpie it looked cool. Jim had written for Rolling Stone so he got some big photographer to take my picture. The title was the irony of the leash. I wore a black turtleneck and I had a rope which sort of went around a corner so it looked like I was tugging something pretty big but you couldn't see it. You could only see the stress on my face. I thought this was a great cover but Jim lost the photograph so Steve Levine drew a cover and it was very high school like the kind of detailed drawing you would do on your notebook. I remember another manuscript that had a sticker on the outside that said hey ted and alice what do you think about Sappho's boat. That manuscript was amazing because I had submitted it for a grant and Muriel Rukeyser had been a judge and I got the grant and she wrote on the manuscript should be published. MR. Holy shit. And she died. Eventually I developed a system of filing in which every year the good really finished poems would get slid into a binder for that year and I could see the growth of my art. I just had a pile of these binders and I kept them in a milk crate under the bed. Sometimes they would move into the file cabinet I found on the street. I'm not trying to be charming. It's just a fact. My whole world laughed at the notion of found poems since everything in our world was found. I think for a few years the poems in the binders would move around my home variously but never went out. My poems were like a little shut in in this condition I mean the kind of permanent record of what I had done apart from books and magazines which I was always avidly sending my poems to. It was shit in the early years. Some guy would say you sound lonely. I think I have told that story before but it's true and I don't think any man has ever received that response from an editor but women always do despite my often resistance to even being considered female that's what you think I am and I buy a cup of coffee and you say ma'am. This is going well. What am I reading lately. Tristram Shandy which is foolish and rhythmic and the Koran which is ecstatic and smart. I was sitting on the plane the other day reading the Koran. That felt great. The first section is called the heifer though I don't know why yet. And uncannily I was also reading a journal my dog subscribes to called Livestock Weekly and it had heifers too. To read about ranching and cattle raising is to experience the enormity of the slaughter which is life. I remember showing someone my box of poems and they said don't you have a copy. And I gleamed no. I liked the perversity of the original. I would never lose this. There's no double. It's the once. When I got a poem perfect for years I would destroy the draft. I don't have space and I don't have time.

Stuff of course was in books. But this was good. How it fell. I expected all the usual things and they have happened. Around fifty I became a college professor. It came and bit me on the ass. There are places where only certain poets read and for me one of them was UCSD. Chiefly because of my friendship with Rae which I've always thought of as a relationship of class. I love her work but I think it's very important to us both that we came from working class backgrounds and we know it. I think with her it creates some aspect of her knowing. How she's curt and jumps in her work. For me it's language purely I think and how I don't mind losing you at all because the story is simple and it's all sound. I remember every poem I ever wrote. I can't recite them but they come back like waves because they are a part of my brain. They are how I have a brain. My brain is inside out. Poetry proves me. I don't give a shit what happens now. Adam was talking about forgetting the other night and I think it was a Lewis Hyde thing—there's the Germanic which is somehow material like lost and the Greek which is more akin to vanishing, either becoming abstract or being covered, paved over, invisibilized.

On the phone I said oh I'm Germanic. Adam said all his poet friends jumped on "the Germanic" but in the days since I'm thinking how Greek I am, thoughts fading into the ether if I don't write them down, forgetting is not stuff, it's the act of once holding information or fact or emotion (in my brain) and then slowly inevitably it drifts away, the void quickly being filled, by the new idea so to speak if the old thought is there at all.

When they wanted me to come to San Diego they did the most marvelous thing which is they moved me. They picked up all my worldly goods for 5000 bucks. When I went back of course there was no big truck and for a while I knew exactly what it cost. About the same. It happened in dribs and drabs. I liked that the truck happened once. It was so cool. We went out and bought a house first so we could tell the truck where to go. They bought me the house which is sort of why I wanted the job. Such an offer. Don't you want my papers too? In New York I had already made the acquaintance of Bill the archivist of the beats. I mean I knew Allen. And the thing about the poetry world is once they all get dying you could become anyone. I had Allen's love, I am truly part of that family as well as several others but I'm not sure I can honestly travel to Iceland as one of the beats. Though I have. Now I was about fifty I was ready for the big kill which is to sell my papers. It means all those scraps and notebooks and recordings and binders and crap. They had such a collection at San Diego in the library and there was some thing about them having to buy them *before* I was hired and they didn't seem particularly interested which felt a little insulting. I felt like they were hiring me because I had energy and could do things but I wasn't exactly the right kind of poet. I asked Bill what he thought and he said wait. He didn't think I was old enough yet. And my friends who had sold to San Diego and Stanford hadn't gotten that much and I thought that I could get more and I was right. So I waited. The uncanniness of going to California with my everything was that along with everything for the first time my box moved. And by now I hope it's clear I mean the box of poems. That milk crate. I have told this story at least once on stage holding a milk crate. It went well. I have been tearing my apartment apart looking for the notes from that version but they are nowhere to be found. It was only seven minutes long and frankly I think this recitation is about four times longer than that. I may regret including this here. I think the idea about the milk crate presentation was that it would be a television show. I also considered popping that screenplay in here. It will probably wind up in my archive. By then I had published quite a lot of books and of course now I was thinking about the big book. You have your retrospective as a poet which is your selected. People outside the poetry world always call it the collected. They don't know the difference and you sound like a twit if you said selected every time they say collected but I do do it sometimes. They have no idea what it is that we do. It sounds like a lot of filing.

I had a long office in the outside of the house in San Diego I mean like down in the yard and I faced a canyon.

The binders were in a drawer in one of the new legal sized file cabinets. A kind of death like me sitting in my office at school thinking preserved, preserved.

There was something tragic about the whole damn thing. I got the house and my girlfriend got classes to teach they so respected our relationship but it atomized almost right away so the whole effect of permanence even the swaying bamboo that I planted felt sneering. Permanence was the worst and yet when I was young I liked to secrete that one final copy of the perfect poem destroying all the drafts and now I began to take them out one by one to make my selected.

I mean it was pretty obvious. Elisa asked for poems to translate for a volume of American female poets in Italian. It seemed like the perfect request. Italian was the true measure of something. I am hesitant to say beauty. But after I made that selection I had the pith. And I began to fatten the thought, and the selection wavered for about seven years. It was about saving my past but uncannily it was about destroying it too.

I read Moyra's book where Mary Wollstonecraft's placenta did not come down so the doctor stuck his dirty hand inside and pulled it out and that's how she died. It feels relevant here.

Eventually I got back to New York. There was a little time in Los Angeles too but I knew that I would never love again in California. The choice was academic or military. I'd rather military but it just never happened. I liked my life in California for a while. Then my dog died. My life was so tragic I bumped into a plant in the backyard one day trying to mow the lawn and I said sorry tree and that became the title of a book.

They bought me a house and they bought me a truck. I'm thinking about San Diego still. I drove east in that truck. I had lived in LA for a couple of years.

I went back to New York and slid the milk crate under the bed.

I stopped in El Paso on the way and we (now myself and a cat, Ernie) stayed with the Byrds, the coolest family in the world, who have a press, Cinco Puntas. Their neighborhood somehow resembled the one we'd just left in San Diego. Brown hills surrounded us, cats walked in the suburban street. Ernie danced around the house staring out the windows. Sure Ernie doesn't want to stay here drawled Bobby. No he's going to New York, sorry. A couple of years later he did wind up moving west and lived till the end of his life with them. He hated my girlfriend, he hated New York. Ernie was an outdoor sort, a member of many families, a man of the street and New York sitting on a windowsill when the world went green in the spring for him was fucking hell. If it was out there he needed to be in it. And he lived and died like that.

All the time I was developing my selected I was carrying it around. I figured there were some secret poems that had never been published and they were in there and I would just pluck them out but I just kept writing in the present and I just never wanted to look in that old box of yellowing pages and many romantic fonts. It was heavy. I took it to Cape Cod, I took it to Vermont, I took it to Montana. I had a new girlfriend she was pretty young and there was a nonfiction teacher on the faculty that had us all over for some kind of stew made of venison and I think she thought I was the biggest pervert in the world. I mean come on. Venison stew. But I brought my box of poems there I remember them feeling so heavy like a cat you inherited from a dead person. That kept staring at you. We lived above a lawyer. It was her house but business was bad so she moved into her own basement and rented the house to us while I taught. Before I left she did my will. She wanted me dead. Probably she felt dead living underneath her own tenants. I tried it in San Diego it was bad.

It's so much better fetishizing my life than my writing. I may not attract a biographer but when

I am done I will be done. By the time the selected came out it all felt like dross. I don't know what that means. There was a shadow.

I just know that starting around 1997 there was the beginning of something I think of as the archival moment and before I sold anything I already started to feel the creeping value of the past and the new place the past was playing in the present.

Intuitively I had always known to save things but temperamentally I am the opposite and felt compelled to create instead a radiant hole.

I have one version of reality in which I parked the truck on 11th Street when we came home from Montana. We definitely unloaded outside her apartment first but I think the box remained in the cab and also a big plastic bin of photographs. I thought who would steal this. And I also remember coming to the truck to move it that morning, some morning and the shock of its cab being empty. I don't know if this is true. You know when something terrible happens and you stand there in the wah-wah like the world keeps changing shapes because you can't believe it's gone. Is this a memory or a sensation of loss. A radiant hole?

I believe a street person opened my truck — my therapist says no. A Ford Ranger opens very easily and they carefully lifted out the box of binders and the big bin of photographs, my manual typewriter, a low soft green Hermes, the large ancient Merriam-Webster dictionary that David Rattray gave me — all these are things that to my mind people who break into trucks wouldn't bother stealing. Instead they gently placed my guts on the curb, replacing them with their dirty old backpack and maybe a trash bag full of shit and they hopped into the front seat with a six or some dope and maybe someone to have sex with, climbing out with their stuff before dawn, the milk crate and bin of photos just staying there ready to be picked up as garbage. Sometimes I see a squatter poking through my binders in the box next to the black trash bags discovering poems and took a pile inside and pasted them on the wall so there's a room in the east village today about ten years later wallpapered in my shredded yellowed poems.

So in 2015 just before I went to Texas for a month I had a conversation in New York with a man named Chris. He was an agent for archives and he said well what do you got and I told him about the notebooks dating back to 1960 and all the posters from readings and performances and videotapes. Any pictures. Well. Yeah though it's kind of weird and I told him how I *had* a collection of archival photographs of myself and Andrei Voznesensky on a couch as he was putting the moves on me; Adrienne Rich and I hugging at some reading and there's captioned photos of me by Allen Ginsberg and even outtakes from the Mapplethorpe shoot. Great, said Chris.

But I don't know where they are. There's this box and then I described the poems in binders in the milk crate. It's weird I said but I'm not sure where those two things are. I mean I've got to have them. I remember in the past people saying and you don't have a copy. No I proudly smiled because I would NEVER lose it. I hadn't considered forgetting where it was.

Can you find them he asked. I think they are either in my New York storage space or I guess I still have one storage unit in San Diego. A place called Big Box. I smirked. He totally was not interested in the details. I mean they could be there but that doesn't make sense. I'm talking to myself. I was thinking of all the trips meaning surely the box was *somewhere* on the east coast. I saw it here. I saw it there.

He paused for a moment sipping his drink. He was thinking about the box with the binders. Or maybe it was the photos. We were in a place on Lafayette called Saint Ambrose. I liked it here I said when I sat down. I do too he smiled. Now he looked up at me. Do you have someone who can look out there. You need to find it. Yeah Mark. I can do that. He nodded thinking. We have to eliminate all the possibilities. In my business, he said, we call a box like that the gusher.

In Texas on that first trip I talked on the phone with a psychic Tarot reader from Tucson. She said it was very close. I just had to write a letter and send it to everyone who ever came in contact with the box in the time it was travelling with me. People were heartbroken. Are you sure it wasn't in your apartment. Are you sure it isn't in *hers*. My girlfriend had a big old apartment she grew up in. It was kind of a railroad. There was this hall she called the closet, but it was more like a long clothes rack with very high shelves. I went to a psychic in New York and he told me she has it. She may not know she has it. I asked her and she said she was very sorry but she would never lie about something like that. I had had several assistants and one got very defensive. She was no longer in New York and she kind of snapped. Are you accusing me of something. No no I have to ask everyone. She gave me her ex boyfriend's number who had a very big closet in the apartment where she used to live. She used my truck sometimes for film shoots. I imagined her unloading my boxes into her home. No I'm sorry he said. It took a couple of days but he looked. I talked to a hypnotist who said she saw something green like a lamp something high. No actually she led me into a hypnotic state and I looked around up there and that's what I saw. There was that apartment I took in LA before I left. I had it for about three days and then I asked for my check back. I was moving to New York. They had this weird storage space that was actually right on the street and I remembered locking and unlocking it and I am pretty sure the box was right in there. I remember talking to some comedian who lived there after me and he said I'm sorry I don't have it.

There was the summer we lived in three different houses on cape cod and three times we moved out. Was it three or was it two. There was a big place in Wellfleet. It was like a duplex but we only lived in half. It was amazing that the house had a dark side you could slip into and have a secret life but you really wouldn't want to. It was all books. It was a used bookstore that closed and this is where he left it. I asked him but the box wasn't there. The other house had a great yard and we had two small dogs by then. My girlfriend said the house had mold. I kind of remember putting boxes down in the basement.

We left suddenly because of the mold so they could have felt they had reason to throw the box out. But they kept my deposit. You don't have a copy. You never made a copy. Nope.

When her and I broke up I was living in Europe for a while. It meant that that assistant Tom had to go to her apartment and move out my stuff. The tee-vee show about my life or this episode of it begins with her framed by her door at the top of the stairs and him taking stuff down the steps and texting me in Ireland. Lamp? No. I asked about books. Any of the plays of Michael McClure. I am obsessed with the Beard mainly because I left it in that apartment I lived in for a while and this was my writing studio. But I think I actually wrote there. This was just always home. That assistant Tom made me really mad. There was a couple of things but once we were having coffee and I queried him about what he remembered when he was taking stuff out and putting it in storage and when he realized the direction of my questioning and the object of my search he laughed out loud.

You're not going to find it he roared. I wrote him a recommendation for graduate school but I don't want to talk to him anymore. I can't tell you how many nights just as I am falling asleep it suddenly flares up into my imagination and I'm flat out on the beach of loss like a story I never understood until I got older. I'm older now. I didn't sell my papers through that guy because it was too painful for sure. He valued them exactly. He felt it and for me the feelings were too relentless then. The next guy cared so much less. What he addressed was my anxiety so I sold it with him. My archive.

I have so many theories. When we were on cape cod the ceiling of my apartment caved in. My friend Nate was staying here. I guess they were working in the apartment above me and weren't very careful. He said he could even see the worker's head upstairs through the hole. It finally got so bad here with the noise and the dust he abandoned ship. First he left the two cats here that I had with that girlfriend. We had two little dogs and two wild cats. It was too much. Then he took the cats out somewhere. Around that time we returned. But the workers had access to my apartment and they could've been throwing out my stuff. Is it possible. Sometimes I think they're in the basement. Ugh. Rats.

There was one more theory what was it. Bedbugs.

My girlfriend had had them a couple of times in her building so when she saw the bloodstains on the side of the mattress she freaked. It was our blood. We did a giant purge of the apartment. Putting things in trash bags getting the place sprayed and then throwing out a ton of stuff. Her building had one of those cement dungeons right below the street where you dropped your trash and we had filled that entire dungeon with black bags. I am always ready to have less so together we went on a binge. I remember the couch that I used to read Bleak House on in the morning. That went out first. She had this extra mom because her own mom had been irresponsible and this woman named Sally helped us clean and lug the mess down. I mean if you date a significantly younger person especially if you are the same age as her parents and her parents' friends it's like you're John Wayne Gacy. So I find it very easy to imagine Sally sliding my box into a trash bag and throwing it out. And why not the second one too the giant plastic storage bin full of worthless photos from another relationship I had gotten stuck with in the end and thought one day I would go through them and pick out the photographs of value but I wound up putting my own mega valuable archival photographs on top at some point. If she slid one box into a trash bag she could easily slide another too. This is the kind of thing that makes you entirely paranoid. She was a nice woman. She wouldn't do that. Who knows. Few people really care that much. She just didn't look at me a lot. Eventually I contacted everyone I knew. I sent them the letter. The second psychic said he didn't find things but he knew somebody who did do that and he would give me their number. But then he got cancer. And then he got better. He was pretty good. By then I was as much asking about the woman I was dating as anything else. And this was somebody else by now. I wrote a pilot about the box because she said if I didn't do that she would. So I did and I showed it to her and she said the format was wrong. I got busy and the next time I talked to psychics and astrologers they didn't think the box was close anymore.

It became my thing and it's been my thing now for probably ten years. I mostly don't tell people. I went to Palestine in 2017 on a tour of five cities with American writers and British writers several of middle eastern extraction and a few Jews. In Palestine I met writers and lawyers and human rights people and every night we read our work and I was at this party one night in Ramallah and I just spontaneously started telling this filmmaker, a woman about my age I figured she'd get it and she laughed and said it's gone and it's wonderful. Somebody else will find it. It's not your problem anymore. She seemed positively gleeful and it weirdly relieved me momentarily and we both walked back into the party.

In Afterglow, my dog memoir of 2016, I had this problem which I wrestled with for the length of the book. Afterglow documented the life, death and after life of my pit bull Rosie but in 1999 almost two decades before the book appeared and about seven years before I was even writing it I kicked out a short piece of writing which I unthinkingly titled "fakir" which means holy man. The piece was a letter from my dog's lawyer in which the lawyer implied I had abused her and now Rosie was suing. The letter seemed like part of a book though the book the piece suggested was funny and arch and I am not that writer. I have my moments but that's about it. I do write longer things but it's always a jigsaw of mood, not *a* mood. I sometimes wish there were thick black lines in writing. I want to make a divider that says nothing, but merely does.

_____

Because I am about to talk about something that happens in my writing but then I had a wave of discomfort about the entire category of "my writing." I should be comfortable with it by now (I mean in this piece or in my life) but I'm not. It just becomes such a thing and it's like your relationship or your mother or your alcoholism. I've always noticed the "your" construction. It's kind of a smarmy thing. The instant it exists the subject feels stale or old. It's like when people from your past or who just haven't seen you for a while sidle over and say—hey Eileen, you still doing *your poetry*. How's *your writing* going. It's kind of the same tone as how's that *relationship*. How's your mother? Oh she's dead. Is your drinking—well how is your drinking? Oh you stopped—well that's good.

We have these spheres we are commonly identified with and it's always prefaced with "your" like this thing of you you just won't stop asserting and so obviously the world in a variety of ways will begin to assert it back. And then you're supposed to chime in. It feels a little gross (because I'm not a man?) like there's this sauce I'm always pouring over the world like that can of paint in the Sherwin-Williams ad: Sherwin-Williams covers the world and there it is happening right before you — the bucket is tipped, the contents spilling all over onto planet earth, glug glug.

I think this ad preceded the moon landing. So the moon landing didn't actually create the concept of the "whole earth." Sherwin-Williams did! In part the ad is effective cause it's a good drawing, it's a cartoon. The covers the world part, the caption, is the redundancy we've come to expect from the world. Just in case you didn't get it the first time I'm going to sum it up for you. I suppose the ad's a little colonizing, which is kind of the problem with "your." Your anything. It's self colonizing. "Your writing." It's not *exactly* "literature," it's thick, it's kind of "other" somehow.

Metonymic, a growth, it's more like habit. The interviewer turns to you after looking at their notes. "So . . . about your writing you've said somewhere . . ." and you are being thrust into the position of being a specialist on "your work" and probably asked to expand or back up some claim you made in the past probably off handedly about it being an alibi, or a little house, it's just some form of mental illness, though it's "my mental illness," you say proudly, one I built for myself. Yeah it's just a form of employment for the unemployable, a life-long something for the got nothings, it's just what I did (shrug) while I was living in this cheap apartment, and while you're here let me tell you about my cheap apartment . . . my love, my dog. I don't like to ever stay on the it of it too long, I mean is there really an it.

I think of writing, at best, as always quickly darting off into what it does. The horizon of the practice. That out there. And even if the subject is "me" it still feels that way. I'm gone. Necessarily.

What I wonder a lot is why everyone who reads doesn't start writing at some point. It just seems like the obvious nervous response. They all want to, many do. Bruce who just put in the electrical panel for the little house told me his wife writes. She's been working on one for ten years he chuckles. That's nothing I smiled back and hand him a copy of my dog book. What's your wife's name. Joy?

It's like when my father taught me to ride a bike. He had his left hand on the crossbar and the other on my back and I held onto the steering wheel. Keep pedaling he yelled and suddenly I was darting into the future and my father was gone. I was riding by myself. So I am. Nobody would think that was a sad moment, in fact so many of the most exhilarated moments of freedom in my life early on were with him. Bunched up on the floor of the roller coaster holding on to my father's legs and feet, screaming. But next time I sat up.

I was young but I thought if this is my death I want to see it. And what I saw was the world. Which is where we are and maybe we can change our pace for the moment.

Because I am feeling a connection now to what is actually one of my favorite fetishes in writing. I'm thinking about that extraneous piece (like the letter from the dog's lawyer) that wiggles its way into something larger and survives.

It's kind of a plucky orphan, a baby virus, and it's what everyone remembers about what you wrote cause it's funny and it's funny and because it doesn't belong. Flash and that's your life. And then everything belongs cause you're dead. It just is.

The problem in the dog book was fitting this unlike piece about my dog suing me into an otherwise book. You see now that I don't really mean to go on about my writing but I will. One of the reasons I write is to give voice to those less privileged (to the voiceless!) and I have mentioned my dog already and now I would like to acknowledge that I also feel a responsibility to write for puppets. I have five puppets in my life, they are not ten feet from me in two small cardboard boxes on my desk. They deserve better.

Their names are Oscar, Bedilia, Montgomery, Crocky (the crocodile) and Casper.

I am writing on the kitchen table at this moment which is pretty much a desk too. A desk with fruit. A desk with vitamins, legal paper, a Christmas postcard from David Beebe & Hilary, newlyweds, and their dog Duane who happily is giving us profile. Let's face it everything is puppets. Certainly in my view.

These puppets were in a road movie we shot about a year ago (can I admit here that Crocky's singing voice is John Ashbery) in Marfa and the film ("The Trip") for me was a realization of my ongoing desire to include the puppets in my work. I made them when I was nine at a CYO (Catholic Youth Organization) puppet making class with a wonderful teacher, Miss Ursula, and in my film one of the puppets helplessly mimes Miss Ursula's German accent and that puppet's name is Casper. The Casper thing is funny since we think it's a cartoon thing, Casper the ghost, *I* thought so, but it's a German thing, there is always a Casper puppet in German puppet theater so it's old. It's a traditional thing. And Casper's very white.

We had puppet shows in my neighborhood when I was a kid and this was another of the activities that predicted my life as an artist. Or merely underlined that I already was. Kids are simply artists if not art. So when I was writing the dog memoir and wanted to give Rosie voice after her life in an authentic way I thought omigod if the puppets had a talk show and invited her on as a guest then *everyone* would have their say. Okay so now we're coming around.

Way back in the beginning of this (For Now) there was a boat reference and coming around is part of boat language. The English language is extremely boaty.

The letter I had summoned or received from Rosie's lawyer could very naturally be thrown up on the screen during the show as an element of quickening. Oscar, the lead puppet who was hosting the show, could read it aloud to demonstrate Rosie's complaint. The letter would be held by the scene and the scene held by the book. It's the moment of transition. The embrace! The imaginary letter henceforth made the show seem real and the real show would validate the letter. Once I slipped it into the script all its power became abundantly clear. And now I could slap it right up front in the book and create a little myth around it, a lie. And then I even got someone[1] who had good/bad handwriting to draw an envelope and address it to me as if we needed even another layer of authentication. Writing is really a crime! *If* so many things in the book like the dog talking and the puppets talking were in fact an invention, a kind of giving that refers to the true thing you ultimately get to espouse in a dream (art) instead of being burdened with having to assure everyone of its veracity (business, news) which we all know now and generally have begun to assume is a lie. Or just an energetic shove of any kind that's purporting to be information. What I mean is that if the puppets are fiction and so is my dog then I can be fiction too. For one brief hairy moment it's not "my writing" cause I'm not real, I'm alive. In my writing!

So what I did finally is made up a story about the letter from the lawyer coming in the mail and

---

1. Mud Howard

the book sat still for a moment and looked. It was real. It was true. Like a play.

Like the moment I was suddenly pedaling madly now was occurring in the writing of a book which I think of as a network of smaller and bigger rotations producing a realistic thing, a state, a place, something anonymous and still that actually becomes porous and now other things i.e. other texts and pictures can also migrate in and become citizens of the world of the book. These outer texts becoming inner produce kind of a bump like I referred to in sound recordings before, you can tell by the different fabric of this writing or assertion that it's definitely not from here but that difference makes here real. In a way I think it's when writing becomes a political act.

Reversing the in and the out. And that's what I want a lot or most in writing. It's when I'm alive. It's not my writing. I'm a puppet. But my own. My own puppet. I think I've made it clear that I never wanted to be a writer. Because I hadn't seen one before! It partly explains the phenomenon of the book Little Women. There's a female writer inside and outside the book. It proposes for a moment that the female writer is real.

Yes, I felt invisible as a kid, insubstantial, flimsy, untrustworthy. I thought that certain professions would make me matter and for a while those ambitions were science and action sports like being an astronaut. I won't relegate those desires to just fantasy, because people do actually get in rockets and fly into space but I didn't become one of them and slowly in my twenties and with a deepening of conviction since then I discovered that to be real was an interior project. The actions you felt inside, the stabs and constant pedaling, practiced and eventually moving out into the world like this thing that I'm writing are the eventual visible practice and it sounds like me and it looks like me changing shape for a very long time and then voila a book. It's a whole other thing to become a person but that's not what I'm talking about here. That's not what I was asked.

And my whole way of doing this therefore is laden with the ambition for the product to have a lot of world in it, be a little humble messy and dirty, so that people can enter like they walk into a building, a public building that is there since once I'm done it's theirs. I vanish into it first but then you do too.

I guess it's "my writing" but really it's a common practice. That's my dream.

*

In fall of 2018 I was contacted by a woman from a Spanish magazine for whom I had written something before. The last experience went well. I liked what I wrote, they did too and they paid me decently and quickly too. So even though I was very busy I said yes.

What she wanted was something about archives. Yawn. Everybody is so into archives. But I had just sold mine to Yale. As a younger poet you know that there's about three ways you will ever make money as a writer. Big grants, big ass grants like the ones the other writers got the day I gave my talk, or on the off chance that when your parents die they have something, anything. My house in Texas was cheap but my mother dying paid it off.

I've seen a number of poets often quite old leave their rent stabilized apartments when their parents die and buy something. Hannah Weiner did it. That was a moment in the neighborhood for everyone. And selling your papers. We all know who got what as in how much money from which university, which universities do sell papers and then poets like to sneer at one another for the strange items that wind up in their collection.

Apparently Allen who got a million from Stanford included a pair of old sneakers in his. And with the money he got a great loft on fourteenth street and he left the poets building on 12th, where he had lived for such a long time in two apartments, one for home and one for office and his presence always made the cred of all of the other poets in the building be so sterling like he made the neighborhood shine for the rest of us while he lived. Allen got a loft and the British poet Thom Gunn actually sneered in a poem about Allen Ginsberg selling Stanford his collected sneakers. Like the sneakers were all. It was snide.

Here's the piece I sent to Spain in 2018.

MY SECRET

As of fall, 2017 I am interred in the Beinecke collection at Yale. What that means is that all of my notebooks since age ten are now being sorted and filed and made available to some part of the researching public. On the occasion of being interred I read at Yale this fall and next fall I will give a talk entitled "How to Write." When I gave the reading at Yale I stayed at a hotel called The Study at Yale. I drove so I handed the keys to my car to the valet and I didn't see it again for a couple of days. I was very tired having driven that morning from Newark airport. I had left my car there for a few days while I read someplace else in the US. And now I had driven here. But still this Yale reading didn't feel like a regular gig but more like the portraits I saw in the Philadelphia Museum of Art, actually in the cool climate controlled basement of the Philadelphia Museum of Art in the 90s when I was doing research for a play I was writing about the poet nun of New Spain Sor Juana Inés de la Cruz. The museum had a portrait that was a copy of the only known portrait of her. I wanted to look at it. But to get to it they first rolled out several other portraits of young women with piles of flowers on their heads in white dresses. These were wedding portraits of women who were entering the convent and their portraits had been painted because they would never again be seen by their families. They were each marrying god or maybe a building, the convent. Secretly they were marrying each other. So I felt a little that way about the reading at Yale. The entire enterprise. I was marrying Yale or my papers were or my writing history was. This was the beginning of the end. I read in a very beautiful room on the second floor of the library. It was a building made out of very thin marble. Light came in from outside but not that much light. It was thin stone so it was a little like being buried alive. There was a nice big audience there, all friendly and happy to see my burial. I think sure many of them might have thought I was just reading rather than truly understanding what was behind the ritual. I read from all over my poetry life, young poems, recent ones. My selected poems had come out just a few years ago so I was used to reading from old work but this was different. Now I wanted to do a good full scan of the corpse. People liked it and afterwards I went out with some of the archivists and Karin who is John Ashbery's biographer. I knew John and she did too but differently. She *knew* John. What hell to be a biographer but I guess what purgatory it is to be me, part interred, the rest still alive and creating more fodder to be placed in folders, filed away, to be installed. I love the archivists. They were all smart and weird and spoke about the archivists before them who were *really* weird, one in a likable way and one in a very mean unlikeable way. They talked about no matter how much scholars read about a poet (and this archive is mainly poets, it's a poets' graveyard) what researchers really want to know is who the poet fucked, or what the poet fucked, probably how they fucked. And you know honestly it's one of the main things I write about in my notebooks. My fucking, my needing to fuck, my needing to stop fucking. And I continue to keep notebooks. It's how I started writing and it's really nothing but ironic. I had NO space in my life as a child. It's the trauma of my life. I had a lovely sunny room when I was a child and then my sister was born and I was moved across the hall to a larger dark shared room. My room sat over there across the hall, the bright one, for as long as I lived in the house and now that light held my brother, a boy. He had the sun, he had the privacy. Nothing much happened in there for ten years and then I was given a greasy black insurance company diary. It had a moose head on the cover in gold and it said 1960. And *I* began. It was my place. In about five years I went for the first time in my life on a vacation with my aunt and her family and neither my sister nor my mother nor my brother came. My dad was already dead. It was just me and my aunt and my cousin. I had my own room and my room didn't have a good reading lamp but the hall did so the room was largely for lying naked on my bed like I had never done before in my life and the hall was for me sitting under the overhead light with my latest little diary, say 1963, so only three years later not five and I would write my life into it. I didn't have sex yet but when there was sex *boom* there onto these pages it would go. And I've been pouring for

years. Nobody's going to ask the archivists if I had sex or who I had sex with. I
just received a galley in the mail from a
young writer who admires my work, in
fact in the galley they describe me as their
hero. But they are in fact researching the
writer Carson McCullers. The writer of
the galley is a lesbian and she believes
Carson McCullers is also one so she has
been reading her letters and transcrip-
tions of her therapy sessions and pieces of
her mostly redacted memoir all in search
of the evidence that Carson McCullers is
in fact a lesbian. That wouldn't be the
problem with me. I'm so obviously a lesbian I don't even call myself a lesbian
anymore. I say queer, or trans. I say they
but none of that matters. There just is no
sexual mystery. The researchers will just
be sitting there turning the pages of my
composition notebooks, hundreds of
them, fifty-seven years of them and say I
started having sex in 1965. Did I start
writing about it yet. I guess there are
some questions. My father died in 1961
and I did not write about that. Guess I

didn't think it was worthy of mention. But I suspect I began to write about sex at some point. And then it was just blatantly clear for years. I was having it, I wasn't having it. It was good, it was lousy. We were breaking up, there was no one. There was someone new. On and on for years. If I've made it so easy, what would they be researching. My work? The last woman I dated made me promise I wouldn't write about her. I'm sure she meant don't write about having sex with me. I said no of course not. Then I said well there's actually only one way I can really make that promise. The joke was that I only write about people after we break up. So if she stayed with me forever no problem. But that isn't true. I was always writing about her. In my note-book. And people will be sitting at a table at Yale reading about her. Somehow *that* makes me more comfortable than think-ing of people turning page after page of *my* sex life. And my sadness. My ambi-tion. And my shame. I like thinking that I'm betraying someone else in the future with my notebook rather than the more depressing thought that I'm betraying myself. I began writing to have some space, some privacy and the end result is all those years of thoughts and desires and worries and feelings being baldly open to the world. Overly naked like that first bedroom I was in. Anybody that can flash a university id or a flimsy cover letter from some journal can sit down and be slightly amused and disgusted by my sex life for years. In fact they can do that while I'm still alive. I'm hoarding the last couple of years. It feels like just by being alive and still writing I'm hoarding. This most recent ex could conceivably go and read about herself IF I allow the current notebooks to enter into the crypt with my name on it. But I will not do that. But it doesn't feel the same anymore. The dirty kick of being alone is gone. Sitting on the plane writing into my black and white composition notebook I could really give a shit if the person sitting next to me is reading what I write over my shoulder. I'm *already* writing now as if someone is reading me. Why not that clod right there. I had imagined when I thought about writing this piece about archives that I would pop some of my current journal in right here. Just like a little trailer from my dead future. The girlfriend before the most recent ex was actually very excited about being in Yale, she loved that that was where our love would go. I hadn't even sold my archive to them yet and she was thrilled. It was like she was already in the future in the crypt, more excited about being there with me than the me here we shared a couple of years ago. There was this very beautiful picture she gave me of herself as a young mother nursing her child. There was this big tit the kid was sucking on. And interestingly those tits had been reduced, actually discarded before I ever met her. I had never met those tits. She gave me that photo and I gave that to Yale. Ha I thought. I'll give them your tits. The more the secrets are theirs, somebody else's, not mine the better I feel about the whole thing. And yet something is hidden. What could it be. I will never breathe a word.

Ok it's a little coy but it's almost the end. And the piece was never published in Spanish (or anywhere at all) because the woman had a personal crisis in her life and I never heard from her again. At one point I read it at a reading and then it was new for a while.

How should I say that the ex I mentioned and I got back for the same number of months we were apart and now I think we're breaking up again. I'm here too much, I travel, yeah that was me. *They just can't have relationships they are just so enmeshed in their writing.* The constant pouring, the worrying about pouring, am I pouring trash, I'm just not pouring enough. I came here to pour and I come here too much and she just doesn't like it. She needs me to be where she is.

I'm in my house writing this and they are outside building the shack. It's almost done, it's gone on since October and I'm going to get a little more money when I finish this but not enough.

I'm accumulating piles and piles of words and Jean and now Alfredo who's doing the plumbing have my credit cards and I write them checks every week and nothing's coming in pretty much and it's all going out.

I'm not going to tell you what Erin and I fight about (though I already did) but inside me the fighting establishes this counter churning feeling like I'm talking to her in my head and I'm standing up for myself and then I weaken and simply love her (and my mother was an orphan and she taught me to be an orphan and I just can't stand up for myself cause I don't belong and I'll just be thrown out) and then I start imagining the whole thing working out and I talk to my closest friends about this (and you now) and I went to bed in a tizzy and I didn't sleep well and I woke early and I thought now what. Erin and I were due to talk.

It was so early Jim and Jean weren't outside yet so I grabbed my computer and a legal pad (a habit I acquired from being in charge of the supplies closet at a legal firm. I think I cut that part out. It was pretty good.) and I sat at the kitchen table and made an inventory. There were the checks which was pretty easy to track thanks to demonic Bank of America, my bank. Really?

I counted the hardware store items twice. It just costs so much to build things, materials on and on at the local hardware store and the bigger joint in Alpine. I wrote each purchase on the legal pad and then I used the little calculator on my cellphone and came up with a total. Wow. It's kind of what I knew though it's considerably over the imaginary figure I began with thinking I can do *that*.

Then I thought how much money do I have in the world. I mean entirely. And I figured that out and then I looked at the two together and though it's not great, I'm okay. I actually am.

And they arrived and I spoke about what things were costing and no one blinked an eye. Jean felt she was keeping expenses down and I guess that's true. I called Erin now, suddenly feeling really solid. I know that I (patting chest) am okay and oddly she was okay too as soon as we began talking. She had a plan and she always had a plan and I was for a time, that day, joyous.

I was sitting with people later on and then it came to me, unbidden, and I think it's my secret, and I know it now. The box is gone. It is truly gone and finally I'm alright with it.

ACKNOWLEDGMENTS

I'd like to thank the Lannan Foundation for that first month in Texas; Nate Lippens and Adam Fitzgerald for excellent and wily reading; Erin Kimmel for that too as well as for wit, beauty, and resilience; and everyone at the Beinecke Rare Book and Manuscript Library; Yale University Press, which is John Donatich and Abbie Storch and Joyce Ippolito, all great friends; and the *Yale Review*, especially Meghan O'Rourke and Michael Kelleher, of course; and PJ Mark always and Patricio Binaghi for inspiration.

This work includes some excerpts from my own previously published material. The line of poetry quoted on page 6 is from "No Rewriting," in *Must Be Living Twice/new & selected poems*, by Eileen Myles, copyright © 2015 by Eileen Myles. The excerpt on pages 19 and 20 is from *Chelsea Girls*, copyright © 1994 by Eileen Myles. Both books were published by HarperCollins.